Service Project Coordinator Workbook

Starting with the Basics

Kim David

Project Stella Teaching Resource Center

Dedication

After working with the GIVE (GCSU Involved in Volunteer Efforts) Center at Georgia College & State University for eight years, I learned from some of the best volunteer managers about how to develop a successful service event, project and program. This workbook is a compilation of all the tips and advice I gained throughout my time with the GIVE Center.

In appreciation of the experience I received through working with the GIVE Center, 10% of all proceeds from this workbook go towards the GIVE10 campaign so other students will have the same opportunities and more.

CONTENTS

PURPOSE OF THIS WORKBOOK

The purpose of this workbook is to guide students in creating a service program that will meet a community need and provide meaningful opportunities to a volunteer team.

By breaking it down into very simple steps, students can take practical steps to making their vision a reality.

To get a Facilitator's Handbook or to see if Kim can facilitate your next training, email projectstellatrc@gmail.com or connect on Facebook @projectstellaTRC

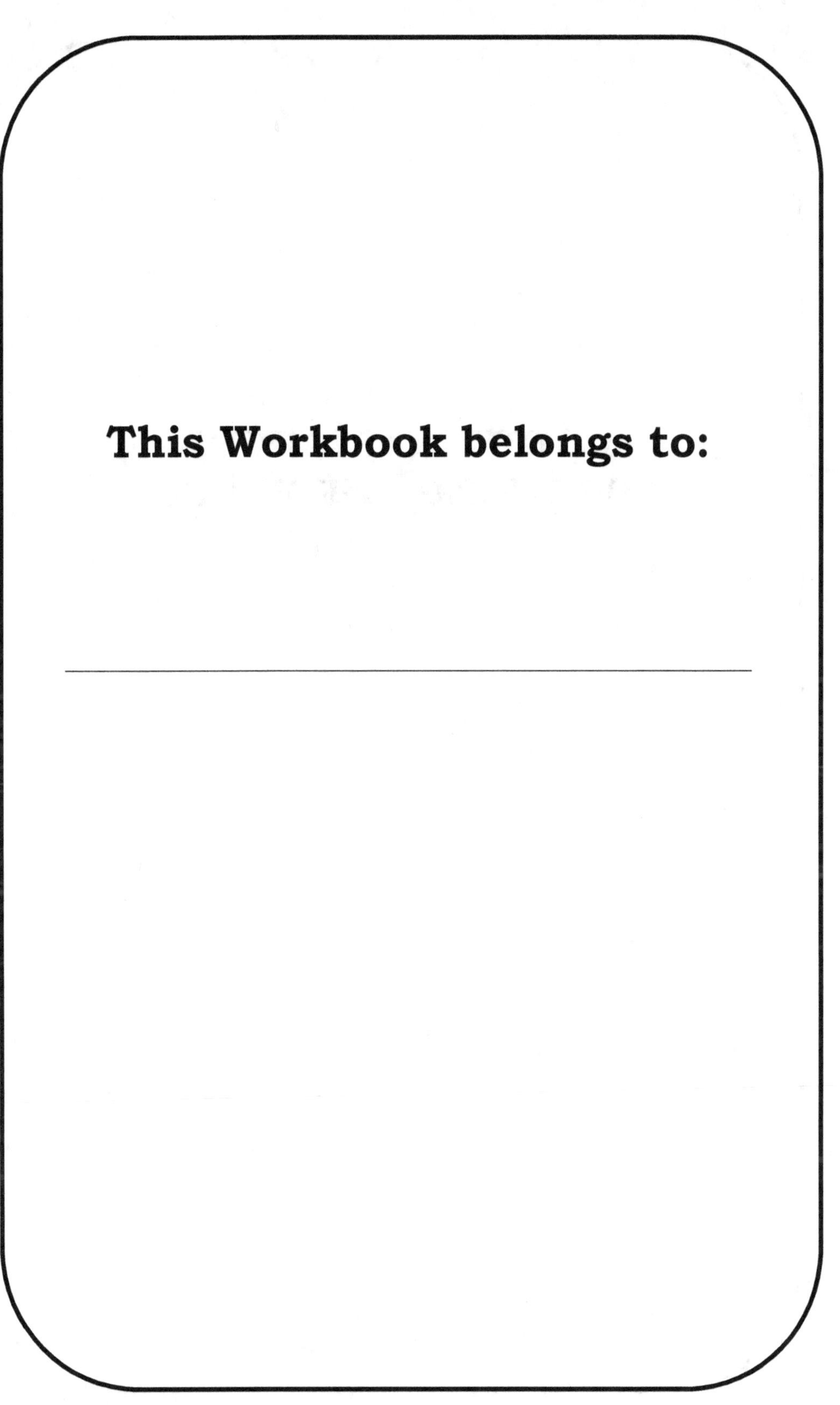

This Workbook belongs to:

____

1 GETTING STARTED: CREATING THE VISION

1 GETTING STARTED: CREATING THE VISION

A Project Coordinator is an individual that is interested in leading a team of volunteers to organize a one-time service event, assist with a service project or develop an ongoing service program.

The very first step a Project Coordinator must take is creating a vision. Without this the project could fail before it begins because there is no direction. Everything a successful Project Coordinator does revolves around this vision. Here are a couple of questions to ask yourself in taking this first step.

When you first think about your project what do you want to do? - Keep this simple!

____

____

____

____

____

____

____

Did you have a hard time answering the previous question? Here are some other questions to help you break it down even more. Eventually, you will be able to use these answers to help create a mission statement (Section 3)

What is a problem in the community you want to solve?

____

____

____

Who/What do you want to work with? (common answers are: kids, adults, environment, animals, teenagers)

____

____

____

____

Now, let's make it a little more specific. Take your previous answer and describe the issue and problem further. (kids that are struggling in math, adults learning to read, animals without a home, teenagers with special needs)

____

____

____

____

How often do you want to do your project? Is it a one time-event/ a semester project or an ongoing program?

____

____

____

____

What do you hope to happen as a result of your project? What you like to achieve? It is okay to dream a little, but know that before the project begins we will need to take a more realistic look at this.

____

____

____

____

____

Before beginning to promote the project or recruit volunteers you will need to have a name for your event, project, or program. By answering these questions you can begin this process.
What are five key words that describe your project?

____

____

____

____

____

Will this project be part of a bigger organization? This could include your campus, community partner, student group, etc.

____

____

____

____

____

List four-five ideas that you come up with. Then ask your friends, families, classmates what they think of when they here each name.

____

____

____

____

____

Did you come up with something that describes your vision and makes sense to the people you asked? If you think you have a name, write it here. You can always change it later but you want to make and changes BEFORE you start publicizing.

____

____

____

2 MAKING CONNECTIONS: BUILDING RELATIONSHIP WITH THE COMMUNITY

2 MAKING CONNECTIONS: BUILDING RELATIONSHIP WITH THE COMMUNITY

Now that you know what you want to do for your event, project or program - you want to make sure that there is a way to do it. You need a Community Partner.

A Community Partner is an organization, school, or non-profit agency that has a common interest in your vision and can connect you with the people or things you want to serve. Sometimes, finding a Community Partner is simple: you want to help kids do better in math and there is an afterschool program at a school needing math tutors. Other times, you might have to be a little more creative.

Answer these questions to help find a Community Partner.

Who/what do you want to serve?

____

____

____

Who typically works with people that have the same interests as you? (Teachers serve kids, Animal Shelters house puppies.)

____

____

____

Is there an agency or agencies that already do what you want your project to do? If this is the case, see how you can support the agency instead of competing with them.

____

____

____

After you have an idea of who you want to work with, you want to communicate your vision to them. In some cases, you might be presenting a new opportunity to them that would add to their existing program. In other situations, they might already be providing the service but you could help expand the amount of volunteers or resources they have to complete their mission.

Is there a resource on your campus that you can talk to about finding your community partner? This could be the office that plans service opportunities for students on your campus or the office that connects with alumni. Think about who does outreach in the community.

____

____

____

____

If you don't have anyone to talk to, do an internet search. Check with your local United Way or HandsOn agency. Contact the Chamber of Commerce. Sometimes the Public Library will also have a list of community resources.

Now make a list:

Agency	**Director/Volunteer Coordinator**	**Phone/Email**

After you make a list of possible Community Partners, contact each one to see how possible it is to do your event, project or program with them.

If you get a "no" that's okay. Just go to the next partner on the list. Don't take it personally. There could be a lot of other factors involved in their answer. But, your chances for a favorable response increases the more you are prepared. Here are some tips to communicating effectively with community partners.

1) **Know who they are and what their mission statement says.** You don't want to waste your time by contacting an agency that has a mission that doesn't align with the type of service you want to do.

2) **Contact during regular office hours.** Community Partners are busy. You might be in a stack of messages and might not be their top priority at the moment.

3) **Contact the correct person.** If they have a Volunteer Coordinator, start with that person first. If they don't - try the Executive Director. In some cases, they might be a one-two person office.

4) **Be courteous and respectful.** You are representing your project. Be the best representative that you can.

5) **Know your calendar.** If you get in touch with a person and they want to meet, know in advance the times you have available. If you say, "Let me get back in touch with you once I check my calendar." - you might miss your opportunity.

6) **Find a connection.** This could be your University, if they are an alum. This could be someone that has already volunteered with them. Having a connection could help you make contact a lot sooner.

3 RECRUITING VOLUNTEERS: DEVELOPING A TEAM

3 RECRUITING VOLUNTEERS: DEVELOPING A TEAM

You now have a vision and a Community Partner. Your next step is finding your team to help make your vision a reality.

You might have this group already together - a student organization you are a member of that is interested in this type of work. If you do, that is great and this will be a much easier step for you. But, other Project Coordinators may have to start at the very beginning.

Here are some questions to answer to help you through this step.

Who of your family, friends or acquaintances have an interest in this cause? Do they have family, friends, roommates, organizations with the same interest?

____

____

____

____

Does your campus have a general service group where members are looking for service opportunities?

____

____

____

Who would your project help get them experience for future career goals?

____

____

____

____

Not everyone who has an interest may be the right fit for your event, project, or service program. Think about what will make a volunteer successful to be able to volunteer with you.

Do your volunteers need to have a specific skill or talent?

____

____

____

List five characteristics you want your volunteers to have:

____

____

____

____

____

What do your volunteers need to commit to for them to be successful? Is this something they can do when they have time available or on a regular basis? Do you need background checks completed? Do they need to go through any type of training?

____

____

____

____

With these answers in mind, where is the best place to find your volunteers? Brainstorm a couple of groups, majors, classes, etc. that you could find students with these characteristics, skills and traits.

____

____

____

Once you know who to "go after", you need to think about the best way to reach them and how you will talk about your project. First you will want to come up with a mission statement and then think of an "elevator speech."

A mission statement is one sentence that sums up what you hope to accomplish with your service opportunity. It briefly answers - who you are, what you do, and how you do it.

Who: ____

What:____

How: ____

An "elevator speech" is a short summary about your service opportunity. It usually includes your mission statement but with more detail. It is a great way to tell volunteers very quickly why they should be participating in your event, project or program.

In three sentences, summarize your event, project, or program:

____

____

____

____

Leaving a Legacy: The worst thing to happen to a program you start is have it be successful and then end once you leave campus. Here are two things to do to ensure you leave a successful program and help with transition.

1) A semester or a year before you leave, find two people who can "shadow" you. These need to be students that express interest and commitment to the program.

2) Create a resource handbook or manual. Have all the contact information of community partners, signature events, and common questions.

4 CREATING BUZZ: PLANNING WAYS TO PUBLICIZE, FUNDRAISE, AND GAIN SUPPORT

4 CREATING BUZZ:
PLANNING WAYS TO PUBLICIZE, FUNDRAISE, AND GAIN SUPPORT

Publicity is all about getting the word out. There are many different reasons why you might want to publicize your service opportunity. Through publicity you can: recruit volunteers, advertise an event where you need community members to come, and try to get donations to support your project (we'll discuss this on the next page).

Answer the following questions to plan the best way to publicize your event, project or program.

Why do you want people to know about your event, project or program? Do you need more volunteers? Do you want to create awareness about an issue? Do you need community members to take part in the service you are providing?

____

____

____

____

____

Who is your audience? Who are you trying to publicize to? This will direct how you publicize.

____

____

____

____

____

Here are some typical ways people publicize their opportunities. It is very important to check the policy of your campus if you are posting fliers, chalking sidewalks or sending emails.

Social Media -- Fliers -- Newspaper/Newsletter articles -- Chalking -- Setting up a table in the dining hall or on campus -- Speaking to groups or classes -- Emails

Depending on the service opportunity, you will probably come to the point that you need to purchase supplies to meet your goal. You might need snacks or journals or gas for transportation. How are you going to pay for these items? This is when fundraising becomes important.

What might you need to buy to have a successful event, project or program? How much money do you think this will cost?

____

____

Fundraisers: This could be selling an item to make money. Common types are bake sales, candy sales and car washes. You can also do a fundraising competition like change wars, kiss a pig, or pie in the face. There are many websites out there with ideas if you do an internet search. The best fundraiser is one that ties in to your mission and attracts your volunteers to participate.

Sponsorships: People and businesses usually will sponsor events and projects that mean something to them and helps get their name out to others. Most of the times you can ask groups to be a sponsor for a certain amount of money if you commit to publicizing their group in return.

Monetary Donations: If your cause is compelling enough, you can often times ask for monetary donations. People will give if the cause is something that personally touches them or if they feel that it is important for their community. Just remember to send a thank you card!

In-Kind Donations: A lot of businesses or groups might want to show their support but they don't want to hand you a check. In these cases, it is better to ask for in-kind donations. Think about what you might be spending the money on and ask for the item instead. You might need snacks for an afterschool program or prizes for carnival games.

Youth Service America and other grant opportunities: There are also grants out there for youth involved in service to create projects. Check out Youth Service America and GrantStation. Subscribe to their email list. They send updates all the time about new opportunities. Some will provide $500-$2000 depending on how involved the project is or what issue it addresses in the community.

One of the quickest ways to gain support for your event, project or program is to collaborate with another group or organization. This is especially helpful if you are planning a service opportunity that needs a lot of manpower. Collaborations also help increase your publicity because more people have an invested interest in the success.

List three or four organizations have the same interest in your cause:

____

____

____

____

What are some challenges you or your opportunity might face that another organization could provide? Getting the word out, funds, supplies, manpower…

____

____

____

____

____

____

Collaboration is about partnership. How could you help this organization out in return? Why would they be invested in your event, project or program?

____

____

____

____

____

____

____

5 MANAGING PROJECTS: KNOWING THE LOGISTICS

5 MANAGING PROJECTS: KNOWING THE LOGISTICS

You have a vision. You have a Community Partner and a team of volunteers ready to go. Now comes the part that can make the Service Project Coordinator stay awake at night - making sure everything is planned right so the event, project or program runs smoothly.

For me, this is my favorite part - making sure every detail is planned so both the Community Partner and the volunteers know what to expect. This is even more important when you have new volunteers serving for the first time. You want them to feel comfortable so they will come back. If you have a group of experienced volunteers, they will be comparing this opportunity to other projects they have done before.

Here are a couple of questions to answer to make sure your bases are covered. Of course, each project is different so some of the items might not apply to you - but this does cover the basics.

I have included additional pages with these questions at the end of the workbook so you can use this guide for other projects you may do.

Before the event, project or first day of the program:

Communicate to your volunteers -

Where to meet: ____

When to meet: ____

Where to go when you park: ___________________________________

Driving Directions: ____

____

What to bring? ____

What to wear? ____

Will food and water be provided? ______________________________

Do you need to know of any dietary restrictions? _________________

Who to contact if unable to come or will be late? _________________

For the day of the event, I complete this exercise:

I close my eyes and think, "*If I were a volunteer coming for the first time…*

Starting in the parking lot, do I know where to go? Are there signs leading me? How do I know I am in the right place? Is someone going to greet me and tell me what the next step is? Will I be introduced to the other volunteers? I am wearing the correct clothing or shoes? Should I have brought bug spray, sunscreen, gloves or a first aid kit? Do I sign in? Where are the bathrooms? What if I am hungry or thirsty? Should I have money with me? How do I know when we are done? Do I stay to help clean up? Will someone contact me about other opportunities?

By completing that exercise, I am able to make a list of everything I need to do. I encourage Service Project Coordinators to do this every time there is a service opportunity. Even after doing the same activity for months, a new volunteer might show up and having something simple like directional signs to the bathroom could help him or her feel more comfortable and excited to return.

Answer these questions or come up with your own for each time you have a service opportunity:

Transportation:

How will volunteers get to where they need to go?

____

What liability is involved?

____

How far do volunteers need to travel?

____

Who will cover gas?

____

When Volunteers Arrive:

Do volunteers need a sign to tell them where to go?

____

What do they do when they arrive?

____

What if volunteers are early or late?

____

Do they need to sign-in? Where?

____

Do volunteers need to fill out waivers or a photo release?

____

Is there a safe place to put purses or bags?

____

Are there extra supplies if a volunteer forgot something?

____

Other Logistics:

Who will tell volunteers what to do? Is there an orientation?

____

____

Do you have someone taking photos?

____

Are there snacks and water available? When can volunteers have them?

____

____

Where are the bathrooms? Are they unlocked? Is there toilet paper?

____

____

Do you have a first aid kit? What if someone gets injured?

____

____

Do you need people to help stay and clean-up or load up supplies?

____

____

One the day of an event or project, my mind is usually thinking of fifty different things. I have found that if I keep a **Service Project Supply Box** in my car it usually helps.

Here are some items I typically keep in my box or car:

- Blank Paper
- Pens, Pencils
- Sharpie Markers
- Masking Tape
- Scissors
- Plastic Tablecloth
- AA Batteries
- Extension Cord
- Baby wipes
- Band-Aids
- Paper Towels
- Plastic Cups

6 EVALUATING PROGRESS: TRACKING HOURS AND MEASURING GOALS

6 EVALUATING PROGRESS: TRACKING HOURS AND MEASURING GOALS

Now that you are done with your service opportunity you can breathe a sigh of relief but you are not done yet. Being successful as a Service Project Coordinator requires you to do some follow up work so your next opportunity can be better. Three things go into this: Reflection, Tracking Hours and Evaluating your Program.

Reflection can take place as soon as your event or project has finished. It can happen formally or informally but needs to take place with the volunteers. The purpose of reflection is to allow the volunteers make meaning of their experience. You can also use their responses to help in your evaluation of the program.

Tracking the service hours completed during each project is nice to have for your personal information but is important that you have for any reports, grants, publicity and fundraising that you may do. People and funders want to know the impact they are helping to make. Does your campus have a way to track service hours that are completed by students? If they do - encourage your volunteers to turn in those hours or if you have a sign in sheet - see if the office tracking the hours will accept it. If there is no office tracking hours, make sure you keep up with them yourself. A basic spreadsheet can do this easily or having a file folder that you keep all sign in sheets in can help.

Evaluating your program is an official way to assess if you have met your goals, if the community partner is satisfied, if the community was impacted and if the volunteers are interested in returning. You will want to talk to all groups involved - the community partner and volunteers. Ask them if they have suggestions for improvement. Above all, you need to evaluate how you felt about the opportunity. Do this as soon as possible so you can write down any thoughts you had while the service was taking place.

7 CELEBRATING SUCCESS: RECOGNIZING YOUR VOLUNTEERS, PARTNERS, AND SUPPORTERS

7 CELEBRATING SUCCESS: RECOGNIZING YOUR VOLUNTEERS, PARTNERS, AND SUPPORTERS

I would not be a good GIVE Center graduate if I did not cover the importance of RECOGNITION in this workbook. My mentor and Director of the GIVE Center, taught me the most about recognition and why it is important show appreciation to volunteers.

Recognition serves three important purposes:

1) Encourages volunteers to stay involved - they know they are appreciated

2) Creates awareness about your service opportunity - volunteers will share

3) Attracts others to your group

Answer these questions as you brainstorm some recognition ideas:

Who have you served with that you want to appreciate?

____

What did they do that was extremely helpful?

____

What would they appreciate in return? A heartfelt thank you note, public recognition, a material item, food…

____

____

When is the best time to show your appreciation? Immediately, at the next meeting…

____

____

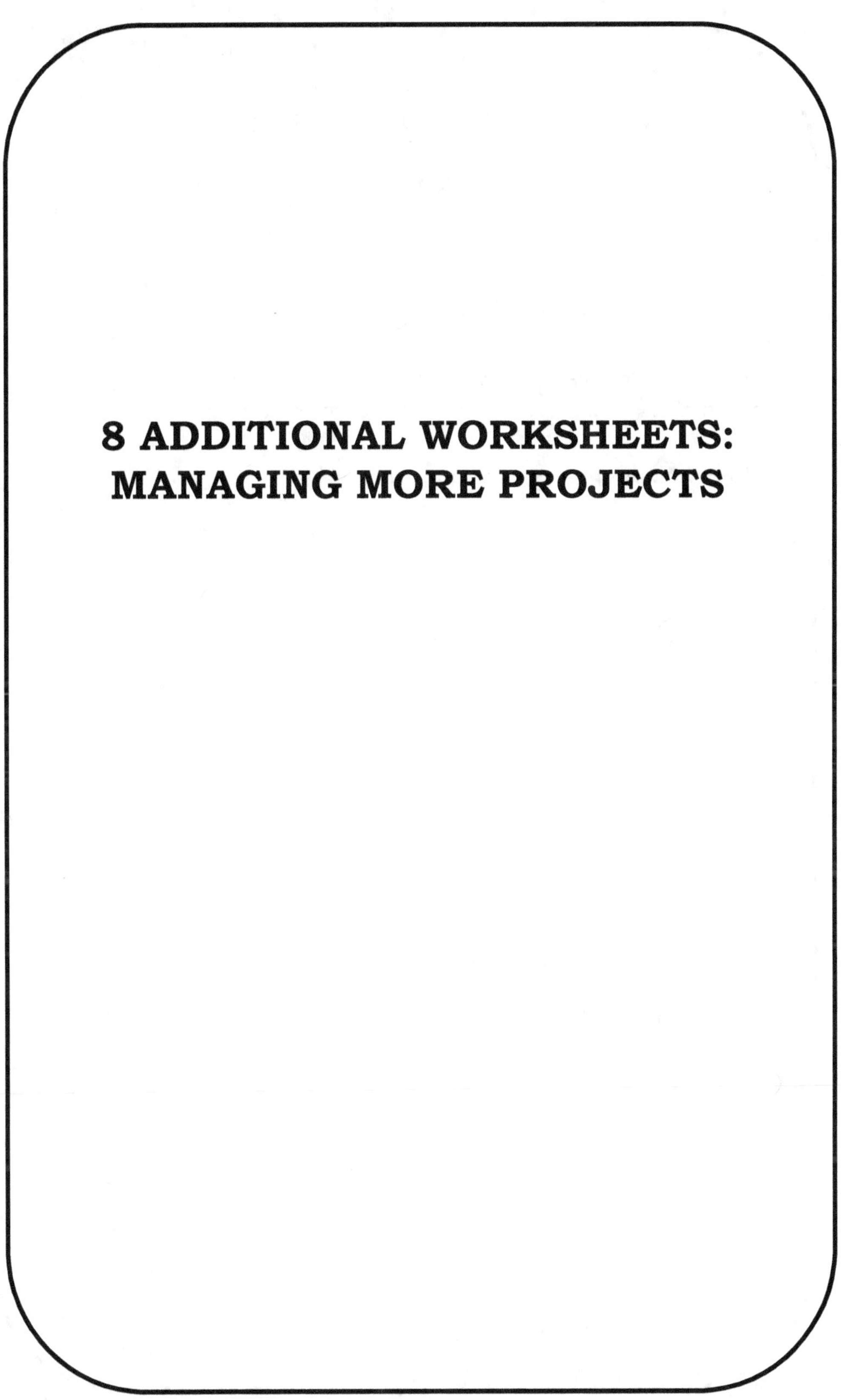

8 ADDITIONAL WORKSHEETS: MANAGING MORE PROJECTS

8 ADDITIONAL WORKSHEETS: MANAGING MORE PROJECTS

Congratulations on completing your first *Service Project Coordinator Workbook, Starting with the Basics.*

These last few pages will help you in planning additional service opportunities. There are five sets of worksheets, three pages each.

Before long, this process will come naturally!

Event: _______________________________

Date: _______________________   **Time:** _______________

Before the event, project or first day of the program:
Communicate to your volunteers -

Where to meet:
____

When to meet:
____

Where to go when you park:

____

Driving Directions:

____

____

What to bring?
____

What to wear?
____

Will food and water be provided?

____

Do you need to know of any dietary restrictions?

____

Who to contact if unable to come or will be late?

____

Remember this exercise: -- *Close your eyes and think, "If I were a volunteer coming for the first time.. Starting in the parking lot, do I know where to go? Are there signs leading me? How do I know I am in the right place? Is someone going to greet me and tell me what the next step is? Will I be introduced to the other volunteers? I am wearing the correct clothing or shoes? Should I have brought bug spray, sunscreen, gloves or a first aid kit? Do I sign in? Where are the bathrooms? What if I am hungry or thirsty? Should I have money with me? How do I know when we are done? Do I stay to help clean up? Will someone contact me about other opportunities?*

Transportation:

How will volunteers get to where they need to go?

____

____

What liability is involved?

____

How far do volunteers need to travel?

____

Who will cover gas?

____

When Volunteers Arrive:

Do volunteers need a sign to tell them where to go?

____

____

What do they do when they arrive?

____

____

What if volunteers are early or late?

____

____

Do they need to sign-in? Where?

____

Do volunteers need to fill out waivers or a photo release?

____

Is there a safe place to put purses or bags?

____

Are there extra supplies if a volunteer forgot something?

____

____

Other Logistics:

Who will tell volunteers what to do? Is there an orientation?

____

____

Do you have someone taking photos?

____

____

Are there snacks and water available? When can volunteers have them?

____

____

Where are the bathrooms? Are they unlocked? Is there toilet paper?

____

____

Do you have a first aid kit? What if someone gets injured?

____

____

Do you need people to help stay and clean-up or load up supplies?

____

____

Event: ___________________________________

Date: _______________________________   Time: _________________________

Before the event, project or first day of the program:
Communicate to your volunteers -

Where to meet:
____

When to meet:
____

Where to go when you park:

____

Driving Directions:

____

____

What to bring?
____

What to wear?
____

Will food and water be provided?

____

Do you need to know of any dietary restrictions?

____

Who to contact if unable to come or will be late?

____

Remember this exercise: -- *Close your eyes and think, "If I were a volunteer coming for the first time.. Starting in the parking lot, do I know where to go? Are there signs leading me? How do I know I am in the right place? Is someone going to greet me and tell me what the next step is? Will I be introduced to the other volunteers? I am wearing the correct clothing or shoes? Should I have brought bug spray, sunscreen, gloves or a first aid kit? Do I sign in? Where are the bathrooms? What if I am hungry or thirsty? Should I have money with me? How do I know when we are done? Do I stay to help clean up? Will someone contact me about other opportunities?*

Transportation:

How will volunteers get to where they need to go?

____

____

What liability is involved?

____

How far do volunteers need to travel?

____

Who will cover gas?

____

When Volunteers Arrive:

Do volunteers need a sign to tell them where to go?

____

____

What do they do when they arrive?

____

____

What if volunteers are early or late?

____

____

Do they need to sign-in? Where?

____

Do volunteers need to fill out waivers or a photo release?

____

Is there a safe place to put purses or bags?

____

Are there extra supplies if a volunteer forgot something?

____

____

Other Logistics:

Who will tell volunteers what to do? Is there an orientation?

____

____

Do you have someone taking photos?

____

____

Are there snacks and water available? When can volunteers have them?

____

____

Where are the bathrooms? Are they unlocked? Is there toilet paper?

____

____

Do you have a first aid kit? What if someone gets injured?

____

____

Do you need people to help stay and clean-up or load up supplies?

____

____

Event: ____

Date: ____________________   **Time:** ________________

Before the event, project or first day of the program:
Communicate to your volunteers -

Where to meet:
____

When to meet:
____

Where to go when you park:

____

Driving Directions:
____

____

What to bring?
____

What to wear?
____

Will food and water be provided?
____

Do you need to know of any dietary restrictions?
____

Who to contact if unable to come or will be late?

____

Remember this exercise: -- *Close your eyes and think, "If I were a volunteer coming for the first time.. Starting in the parking lot, do I know where to go? Are there signs leading me? How do I know I am in the right place? Is someone going to greet me and tell me what the next step is? Will I be introduced to the other volunteers? I am wearing the correct clothing or shoes? Should I have brought bug spray, sunscreen, gloves or a first aid kit? Do I sign in? Where are the bathrooms? What if I am hungry or thirsty? Should I have money with me? How do I know when we are done? Do I stay to help clean up? Will someone contact me about other opportunities?*

Transportation:

How will volunteers get to where they need to go?

____

____

What liability is involved?

____

How far do volunteers need to travel?

____

Who will cover gas?

____

When Volunteers Arrive:

Do volunteers need a sign to tell them where to go?

____

____

What do they do when they arrive?

____

____

What if volunteers are early or late?

____

____

Do they need to sign-in? Where?

____

Do volunteers need to fill out waivers or a photo release?

____

Is there a safe place to put purses or bags?

____

Are there extra supplies if a volunteer forgot something?

____

____

Other Logistics:

Who will tell volunteers what to do? Is there an orientation?

____

____

Do you have someone taking photos?

____

____

Are there snacks and water available? When can volunteers have them?

____

____

Where are the bathrooms? Are they unlocked? Is there toilet paper?

____

____

Do you have a first aid kit? What if someone gets injured?

____

____

Do you need people to help stay and clean-up or load up supplies?

____

____

Event: _______________________________

Date: _______________________ **Time:** _______________

Before the event, project or first day of the program:
Communicate to your volunteers -

Where to meet:
____

When to meet:
____

Where to go when you park:

____

Driving Directions:

____

____

What to bring?
____

What to wear?
____

Will food and water be provided?
____

Do you need to know of any dietary restrictions?
____

Who to contact if unable to come or will be late?

____

Remember this exercise: -- *Close your eyes and think, "If I were a volunteer coming for the first time.. Starting in the parking lot, do I know where to go? Are there signs leading me? How do I know I am in the right place? Is someone going to greet me and tell me what the next step is? Will I be introduced to the other volunteers? I am wearing the correct clothing or shoes? Should I have brought bug spray, sunscreen, gloves or a first aid kit? Do I sign in? Where are the bathrooms? What if I am hungry or thirsty? Should I have money with me? How do I know when we are done? Do I stay to help clean up? Will someone contact me about other opportunities?*

Transportation:

How will volunteers get to where they need to go?

____

____

What liability is involved?

____

How far do volunteers need to travel?

____

Who will cover gas?

____

When Volunteers Arrive:

Do volunteers need a sign to tell them where to go?

____

____

What do they do when they arrive?

____

____

What if volunteers are early or late?

____

____

Do they need to sign-in? Where?

____

Do volunteers need to fill out waivers or a photo release?

____

Is there a safe place to put purses or bags?

____

Are there extra supplies if a volunteer forgot something?

____

____

Other Logistics:

Who will tell volunteers what to do? Is there an orientation?

____

____

Do you have someone taking photos?

____

____

Are there snacks and water available? When can volunteers have them?

____

____

Where are the bathrooms? Are they unlocked? Is there toilet paper?

____

____

Do you have a first aid kit? What if someone gets injured?

____

____

Do you need people to help stay and clean-up or load up supplies?

____

____

Event: _______________________________

Date: _____________________________   **Time:** _____________________

Before the event, project or first day of the program:
Communicate to your volunteers -

Where to meet:
____

When to meet:
____

Where to go when you park:

____

Driving Directions:

____

____

What to bring?
____

What to wear?
____

Will food and water be provided?

____

Do you need to know of any dietary restrictions?

____

Who to contact if unable to come or will be late?

____

Remember this exercise: -- *Close your eyes and think, "If I were a volunteer coming for the first time.. Starting in the parking lot, do I know where to go? Are there signs leading me? How do I know I am in the right place? Is someone going to greet me and tell me what the next step is? Will I be introduced to the other volunteers? I am wearing the correct clothing or shoes? Should I have brought bug spray, sunscreen, gloves or a first aid kit? Do I sign in? Where are the bathrooms? What if I am hungry or thirsty? Should I have money with me? How do I know when we are done? Do I stay to help clean up? Will someone contact me about other opportunities?*

Transportation:

How will volunteers get to where they need to go?

____

____

What liability is involved?

____

How far do volunteers need to travel?

____

Who will cover gas?

____

When Volunteers Arrive:

Do volunteers need a sign to tell them where to go?

____

____

What do they do when they arrive?

____

____

What if volunteers are early or late?

____

____

Do they need to sign-in? Where?

____

Do volunteers need to fill out waivers or a photo release?

____

Is there a safe place to put purses or bags?

____

Are there extra supplies if a volunteer forgot something?

____

____

Other Logistics:

Who will tell volunteers what to do? Is there an orientation?

____

____

Do you have someone taking photos?

____

____

Are there snacks and water available? When can volunteers have them?

____

____

Where are the bathrooms? Are they unlocked? Is there toilet paper?

____

____

Do you have a first aid kit? What if someone gets injured?

____

____

Do you need people to help stay and clean-up or load up supplies?

____

____

Project Stella Teaching Resource Center was founded by Kim David while pursuing her Master of Library and Information Science degree at Wayne State University. The mission of Project Stella TRC is to provide hands on educational resources for teachers, families and community groups.

With the *Service Project Coordinator Workbook*, Project Stella TRC introduces their service-based curriculum with plans to develop more materials for adults, teens, families, and educators to encourage community involvement, awareness, and volunteerism.

Kim David can be contacted by email at projectstellatrc@gmail.com or through Facebook @projectstellaTRC.